BOA
EDITIONS
LIMITED

Sleeping with Houdini

Sleeping with Houdini

poems by
Nin Andrews

AMERICAN POETS CONTINUUM SERIES, NO. 108

BOA EDITIONS, LTD ❧ ROCHESTER, NY ❧ 2007

First Edition
07 08 09 10 7 6 5 4 3 2 1

Publications and programs by BOA Editions, Ltd.—a not-for-profit corpora-
tion under section 501 (c) (3) of the United States Internal Revenue Code—are
made possible with the assistance of grants from the Literature Program of the
New York State Council on the Arts; the Literature Program of the National
Endowment for the Arts; the County of Monroe, NY; the Lannan Foundation
for support of the Lannan Translations Selection Series; the Sonia Raiziss Giop
Charitable Foundation; the Mary S. Mulligan Charitable Trust; the Rochester
Area Community Foundation; the Arts & Cultural Council for Greater Roch-
ester; the Steeple-Jack Fund; the Elizabeth F. Cheney Foundation; Eastman
Kodak Company; the Chesonis Family Foundation; the Ames-Amzalak Memo-
rial Trust in memory of Henry Ames, Semon Amzalak and Dan Amzalak; and
contributions from many individuals nationwide. See Colophon on page 88 for
special individual acknowledgments.

Cover Design: Lisa Mauro
Cover Art: "Houdini's Dream" by Robert Carioscia
Interior Design and Composition: Richard Foerster
Manufacturing: Thomson-Shore
BOA Logo: Mirko

Library of Congress Cataloging-in-Publication Data

Andrews, Nin.
  Sleeping with Houdini : poems / by Nin Andrews. — 1st ed.
    p. cm. — (American poets continuum series ; v. 108)
  ISBN 978–1–929918–99–7 (pbk. : alk. paper)
  I. Title.

PS3551.N444S54 2007
811'.6—dc22
                              2007003734

BOA Editions, Ltd.
Nora A. Jones, Executive Director/Publisher
Thom Ward, Editor/Production
Peter Conners, Editor/Marketing

Glenn William, BOA Board Chair

A. Poulin, Jr., President & Founder (1938–1996)
250 North Goodman Street, Suite 306
Rochester, NY 14607
www.boaeditions.org

Contents

III. THE BEAUTIFUL LIE

This book is dedicated to my beautiful sister, Salley, and to every Houdini whoever lived, who has mastered the art of slipping away or between the cracks and into the horizon without a backward glance. Of course, every escape artist knows the risks. As the French say, Partir, c'est mourir un peu.

I

Making the Sun Rise

Falling

Night after night, a girl dreams of falling. Falling from planes, clouds, swings. Always falling. She has been falling for so long, she can't remember how she ever landed in one world, one town, one farmhouse with yellow curtains, bees circling the ceiling. Sometimes wakened by a callused hand, sometimes sent into a corner, smelling of must and furniture polish *to think about it*, she feels words drift through her like tiny glass splinters. It is only by lying that she can stay alive.

Making the Sun Rise

In those days the girl could make the sun rise. Each day it began as a tiny glow the size of an apple seed in the center of her forehead before expanding, stretching out like melted taffy across the hardwood floor, then crawling up the windowsill and out into the streets. She could feel its white heat beneath her skin as an electric current, leaving her thoughts and dreams as each fragile beam entered the world. She knew it was only a matter of time before others saw her brilliance. After long days of emitting light, she was reduced to cinders, slowly climbing the air. Her mother would appear in the doorway and not seeing her, call out, *Are you in there, Sweetheart?* The girl never answered. Instead, she felt all the empty rooms inside her and someone hiding in every one.

Houdini

Obsessed with Harry Houdini, a mother read her daughter stories about the great magician who slipped out of handcuffs, straitjackets, and underwater cages. Her father said Houdini could speak to spirits, too, and dead birds came back to life, fluttering from his hands and swooping into his audience. Her mother didn't remember Houdini's birds. But she said she'd actually seen him with her own eyes, when she was a child.

The girl saw him too. Each night when she closed her eyes, he was there. A tiny man, trying to escape from a glass box the size of an ice cube. The girl would melt his ice with her hands and hold him like a baby chick, just hatched from the shell. Her mother said Houdini died because a stranger punched him. The girl was sure that he drowned. But her father believed in conspiracy theories. He said no one tells the truth. No one likes a man who can escape every time, who can fool a crowd and perform impossible feats and make the women swoon.

But what if he escaped, the girl asked. What if he slipped out of the water when no one was looking? He became an invisible man and is now living his invisible life in the invisible world happily ever after . . .

❧

The Game

Staring in the shop windows and watching myself pass by, I could almost see her: her hair black, her skin darker. Like toffee, my favorite candy. Maybe she had dark eyes, too, not like the blue eyes of my mother or Mary Rose or Janet who whispered about me in class. Sometimes I tried to dig a tunnel to her when I dug for China in the sandbox. I liked to ask about life before I arrived. My father would make up stories. Once he said I had come out of heaven on a Monday in June, riding a silver bird. I was already speaking another language. After they let me in the house, no one could sleep. He wanted to send me back to where I came from, but my mother wouldn't allow it. My shrieks, he said, could wake the dead. Nothing would calm me. Then one night I went quiet. By morning I had turned into another girl.

Aspirin

The day I ate two bottles of St. Joseph's baby aspirin, my mother was out of town. My father had fallen asleep, watching football in the den. I climbed up on the sink in my parents' bathroom where the mirrors reflected back and forth, back and forth. I could see myself again and again to infinity. There were so many of me present, I called out *Hello!* to every one. No one answered. But when I ate the orange-flavored tablets, so did they. Orange, my favorite color. I ate slowly, singing and waving to the other girls. It was almost a party with so many of us present. I wanted to meet them all, break open the glass and set them free.

When my father discovered me holding the empty aspirin bottles, he didn't scream or spank. Instead he picked me up and carried me outside to his dark Buick. He drove with me in his arms, leaning me back against his chest. It was the way he held me against him, his prickly chin pressing against my head that I remember best. I wanted to be held like that forever. Sometimes, looking at a photograph of my father, I still taste the bitter-sweet orange of children's aspirin. Then I think of the other girls, so many others I might have been, if he'd held them too.

❧

The Invisible Girl

The girl who was invisible knew things. She knew that everyone else was starring in a movie, and her job was to watch. Just watch it. What else could she do? Her skin wasn't even real. It was only the idea of skin. And like all ideas, it was magic. Sometimes it became transparent. Even the birds flew through it, and bullets. Other days it was liquid. When she swam, she was the water. Every now and then she turned into a tree, so heavy and still she couldn't move. Instead she felt the sap run through her veins and fill her with shadows and song.

But there were rules. Always be quiet was one. Don't let on was two. You might be seen then. And not forgotten. Not that her parents meant to forget her when they dropped her off at school, the tennis courts, the local swimming pool. At the end of the day she watched as parents came in station wagons, and one by one the other children went home. Some were hugged by their parents, and some were smacked. Every day a red-haired boy left sobbing after he refused to get out of the water. She didn't envy any of them really. She liked the feeling of being alone, listening to the crickets and watching the moon rise, long after the pool and playground emptied. She liked listening to the lifeguard talk on the phone to his girlfriend, saying *I will be there. Yes. 10:00 sharp. I love you.* She had heard those words before. Her father said words like that every day. She was glad they weren't true. She'd rather stay there forever. Let the world carry everyone else away.

❧

Just the Thing

Rushing down the aisles of Roses Drug and Gifts, a black purse swinging by her hip, her skirt floating around her knees, my mother selected scented soaps wrapped in cellophane, a red rubber thumb cap, and a card of men's shirt buttons. Wheeling her cart around the store as easily as a needle in a record groove, she gathered purchases without breaking stride. She shopped, walked, and talked so fast, my father said she was a 33 album played like a 45. Behind her, I eyed the racks of Easter bunnies, plastic dolls with unblinking eyes, pop-bead necklaces, gum ball machines, and the fish tanks, where children could, for a dime, take home a single goldfish in a Glad bag. I felt that sting of desire for something, anything. *What?* My mother would ask. *What?* I never could answer before the clasp of her change purse snapped shut. On the hot car-ride home, she'd announce *I found just the thing,* while I stared out the window, wondering what that was.

Brown Apples

Wake up, I whisper to my mother. *Wake up.* I want to wake her so slowly, she will think it happened naturally. I blow on her face, and when my mother's eyelashes flutter, I run and hide behind the half-opened door. Then I wait, edge closer and closer to the bed. When I am very close, my mother's eyes fly open. *What are you doing in here?* She shuts her eyes again.

My mother falls asleep as easily as she breathes. She falls asleep mid-sentence, or even mid-bite. My father says my mother is a hummingbird. Hummingbirds, I read, often die in their sleep. One day, exhausted, they drop from the sky into a sleep from which they never wake.

Don't sleep. Please. I lean over my mother, listening for breath. She is older than other mothers. When she sleeps her hair turns grayer. The creases around her eyes and mouth deepen. I don't want my mother old. I imagine dreams like fish, swimming beneath her eyelids. If only I could peer into them. It would be like opening a present I can never have. I see the apple on the bedside table, its insides amber where her teeth sunk in, sticky at the base. A fan hums and hums. My mother wears a pink T-shirt and voluminous underpants that hang loosely around her skinny legs, laced with an intricate design of blue veins.

I place a finger on a single vein, trace the tributaries extending in a thousand branches. Like the rivers on a map I drew for geography class. My mother wakes again, startled, and sits up, tucking her legs underneath her.

What makes blue lines on your skin? I ask. My mother shrugs and bites into the apple. *Mom, don't eat that. It's brown.* My mother yawns and says, *It's fine. If you were in India, you'd be happy for an apple like this. This apple isn't rotten. It's simply oxidized. Inside it's still sweet. In India people know it's not the surface that makes the fruit good.* Then she takes another bite.

Cormorants

The year my parents fought incessantly, my mother took me to the seashore for a vacation. Some good sea air, she reasoned, would do us both good. A friend let us stay in her cottage in Maine. I remember the rocky coast, the salty wet air on my skin. Staring out at the dark water, watching the birds, I listened to my mother who could name each one and tell their stories. Like the Leach's petrel that lives on an island and incubates its egg for twenty-four hours at a time. The speckled seagull that turns white and gray when it's grown. The bald eagle that landed on a dead spruce tree next to our cabin, and my mother said it was so strong it could carry a small dog in its talons. The eagle let me walk close. It looked down at me as if I were tiny, tiny as a fish, and I imagined it lifting me out of the water and into the sky. A crow started cawing until the sky was swarming with angry black birds. Crows don't like eagles, my mother said. So they call the local crow society in to chase them away. But I wondered about the loons and cormorants. *Why do the loons laugh?* It's just their song, my mother answered. She had an answer for everything. *But what about the cormorants? Why do they leave their wings outstretched for so long?* To dry them, my mother said. But one day I watched cormorants in the middle of a downpour, opening their wings, welcoming the rain.

Names

Names, I discovered, have power. But how could anyone choose a name? How could my parents have known which name was mine? Maybe, I thought, it was like knowing which fruit to pick at the market. My mother squeezed each one, sniffed it, then slid it into a plastic bag. In the same way, she told everyone, *Just call me Janet.* Not Jane. Thank God my mother wasn't Jane. Janes are never pretty or popular. Janes have dishwater blonde hair and paper-white skin, and they wear saddle shoes and brown socks every day. They could star in grade school plays about the Pilgrims. But Janet is different. Janet is cute, though not as cute as Elizabeth who wears stockings, even when it's hot. Elizabeth . . . even her name is like the sound of stockings rubbing together and the scent of lemons. Elizabeth sat behind me in class. She dabbed lemon extract behind her ears as perfume, and she combed lemon juice through her hair in summer. Each fall her hair had blonde stripes. I wanted her stripes and her scent of lemons. I wanted a z in the middle of my name and long braids with red ribbons. I wanted to be Elizabeth. Sometimes I wondered. What if I was? What if I was given the wrong name? And now Elizabeth was living my life, dreaming my dreams, wearing my things.

❧

Sweet Tarts

Rhonda Pinston from the fifth grade fainted right off the bleachers in the middle of a choir concert. Everyone whispered about Rhonda Pinston. Rhonda Pinston had big bosoms and pink brassieres and see-through blouses. The boys gave her sweet tarts at recess. Not little sweet tarts that come in packets, but giant ones the size of clams. Grape, her favorite flavor. Rhonda's fingers and lips were always stained purple. There were purple fingerprints on her blouse where she adjusted her brassiere. One girl whispered that Rhonda Pinston fainted because it was the first day of her period. No one would say what it meant to have a period, but it had something to do with bosoms. Everyone got so excited, staring at Rhonda, I decided to practice. After school I practiced fainting in my own room, falling, over and over, my knees going weak, a pillow pressed against my head. Each time I fell, I thought of sweet tarts, giant purple ones, and the boys staring down at me as if I were Rhonda.

Young Ladies

A girl just never knows when her special day will arrive, now does she? But when it happens, she won't smell too nice. I have to warn you. That's why I advise all my classes of girls who might be young ladies any day now to go out and purchase themselves a little bottle of cologne and carry it in their purses at all times, along with some sanitary napkins.

Several times a year Mrs. Pinkerton came to visit the fifth and sixth grade classes, carrying a Safeway bag from which she'd whip out a large box of Modess pads and a slender white belt. Demonstrating how to fasten it, she was our stewardess, preparing us for flight. Mrs. Modess, Rhonda Pinston called her. *Some girls don't bleed for years*, Mrs. Pinkerton would add, waving a sanitary napkin in the air. *Why? Because they don't eat right, that's why. Good food is just so important, especially for young ladies. Raise your hands if you can name some nourishing snacks. That's right, apples, bread, plums and cantaloupe, bananas . . . Anyone else?* I'd listen, picturing all that food like sunlight and water on a plant, causing blood to seep out from between my legs, causing my breasts to grow soft and round. But I knew I could never have a body like that. Just imagining it gave me a disturbing sense. My body, an imposter, beautiful and nude, no longer my own.

❧

Lime Green Teddy

Girls learn better when they are in school with just girls, and they make better friends, too, my mother announced the day she decided to send me to an all girl's school. She said I would remember the girls forever. And she was right. I remember them all, especially Sarah Lee Bailey. For her ninth birthday, Sarah Lee's father gave her nine teddies, not the bears but the silky lingerie, and when Sarah Lee modeled her lime green teddy, she told us her father said she looked just like a sherbet. She looked so fine, he said he wanted to eat her. The next week Amy and Resa bought lime green teddies too. My mother wouldn't let me buy a teddy, but all the other girls were allowed, so I lied and said I had a lime green one. I was fine with my lie until one day in late October when I didn't raise my hand to vote for Nixon. No one could believe it. They called me a liar. *Liar liar, pants on fire.* Sarah Lee felt sorry for me and invited me to sleep over. *Don't tell a soul,* she said that night, *but I think you're really pretty.* Then she kissed me, slipping her tongue between my lips and asked me to practice French kissing so we'd know how to do it when the time came.

Menses

It didn't matter. Nothing did. The day I came home from school with a note, I felt as if I were sitting on a roll of toilet paper. I shifted back and forth. I kept going to the bathroom. I told Maureen. Maureen promised not to tell. No one spoke to me at lunch. No one asked me to play after school. At dinner, my parents didn't ask me why I wasn't eating my turnips and bitter greens. When I left the table and ran upstairs, they didn't call me back. I could hear the lowered voices, as if they were discussing me from below.

The Summer I Turned Thirteen,

July was so sweltering, the pond shriveled into a mud puddle, and polliwogs wriggled in the creek mud where cats swatted them out with their claws. JJ, the boy who died of an overdose later that year, took up helping me in the vegetable garden, sinking in the tomato sticks, weeding the okras and peas and checking our bees. Nights he'd be waiting in the old tire swing. We'd sit side by side, the hairs on our arms almost touching, the two of us watching ants circle a bucket rim and listening to the katydids and tree frogs sing. Sometimes the rain smelled so close, heat lightning lit up the sky where bats swooped. We'd watch them, dive-bombing bugs. They were always falling so fast, I'd wonder how they reversed directions. The bats looked as if they were bouncing on air, as if there were some kind of magic string or elastic, pulling them back to the sky again and again. Or maybe it was down. I was never sure.

Dust

A girl suffers bouts of dizziness. She feels as if she were coasting, as if everything were over long before it began. Often she levitates from her body like dust in the morning air and wishes she never had to descend. She remembers eye operations when she was a girl, the feeling of doctors tightening the strings that hold her eyes in place and tying them like shoelaces. She watches interns lifting her hospital gown and fondling her abandoned body. All over her skin the handprints of strangers keep traveling. When she looks out the window at night, she sees not stars but pebbles hurled into space.

Like This

Sometimes long after someone is gone, I see his face in a passing car or feel his fingers running through my hair, a quick touch or glimpse, nothing more. I'm used to this by now, so used to it I've learned to see quickly what was or could have been.

When I was a girl, my father said that every twenty minutes we vanish, go silent, join the dead and our dreams. If you could time it and knew when to start the clock, you'd see them, too, lingering there between one thought and the next. Some steal a breath of your air or give you a tiny pinch. Others walk right through you on a whim. A sudden chill, a shudder, it's the natural response. Try to stop them if you can, repress or pretend. Say no one's here. You're all alone in the evening air. It makes no difference to them. They know where they've been. And how much they like it, touching you like this, traveling through you again and again.

❧

The Tunnel

Dana is a painter who tries to commit suicide once a year. She says suicide wishes come with a change of weather. By late fall she feels like a train entering a tunnel at reckless speeds. She rushes far below or away, often ending in a mental institution in Switzerland where shock treatments are standard practice. She says she likes them because they work. By midwinter she is ready to reemerge, giddy with tales of near-death experiences and the desire to paint more landscapes. Some of her landscapes are from inside the tunnel with stone walls and rubble, someplace where a bomb exploded once upon a time. She remembers seeing it happen but can't recall how or where. Other paintings are of outside, far above the ground. Their lit skies are the kind one blinks at with awe after staying inside too long.

Max from Berkeley writes love books. He makes millions by telling readers how they need only think rich and beautiful thoughts, and the world will fall in line with their wishes like a trained dog. All you have to do is housebreak your puppy. Matter follows thought. It's cosmic law. Max sends me postcards of ascending nudes and the drowned Ophelia. He sends me smiley faces and swimsuits that turn transparent when wet. Max is manic and lives on antidepressants. Someday, he says, he won't be able to stop himself.

An intern in a white coat strokes my arms, combing all the hairs in one direction across my cold skin. *A pretty body like that,* he sighs. *I can't let you kill it. I save bodies like yours every week and send them back on the streets. Nights I go home to an empty apartment and dream of women who commit suicide. Not one says thanks.*

Thanks, I whisper, but he isn't listening. *Thanks.* Looking at the ceiling, I think of Dana's paintings. The way the sky and the sea appear the same. Sometimes when I stare at them, I can't tell if I'm lying on the bottom of the ocean, looking up at the waves. Or if I'm riding in an airplane, far above the clouds, gazing down at the world below. Sometimes I can still hear my mother calling and calling *where are you, Darling? Is that you upstairs?*

Sleeping for Kafka

I heard on the radio this morning that prayers can heal. Experiments demonstrate that cancer patients who are prayed for, even by an anonymous person, have a better prognosis than those who receive no prayers.

A person can purchase prayers from Grace Church in Kansas by dialing 1-800-prayers. Visa and Mastercard are accepted.

I read that Kafka, a chronic insomniac, felt refreshed after watching his beloved sleep. Sometimes he invited her over, just to admire how she draped herself over his couch, wrapped in immaculate rest.

Some speculate it was the dreams of his beloved he wrote.

Thoughts like dreams drift from mind to mind. Some are heavy and sink to the ground or disappear under water where they grow like sea plants, while others are light and glide upwards like helium molecules.

When Jacob saw angels going up and down a ladder, they were merely tracing his thoughts.

Nietzsche said few people think their own thoughts. Instead they are thought. Many people are dreamt and prayed. They are like seashells inhabited by hermit crabs.

Most of us have no clue whose dream we are.

❧

II
Déjà Vu

Burning Point

Sometimes I know the world is perfect, as perfect as a Mozart concerto, and I want it to feel that way forever, like a tune I can hold inside me, or a warm haze I sometimes felt as a girl when my mother stroked my hair with her fingertips. But something always happens, doesn't it? My mother crying, my father leaving, the screen door slamming behind him. I remember the day I watched Terrence Uchino playing with a magnifying glass, holding it over a dry leaf. At first there was nothing, then a flame, tiny and yellow, eating the fringe, following the edges until the leaf curled inwards toward itself in a gesture of helplessness. What bothered me wasn't the end, the moment of blackening, or giving in to the flame. It was that instant between flame and no flame. That split second when I held my breath and watched for the first flicker of fire, leaping, dancing. How could I predict it? That moment. When everything changed.

Nightmare

As with every dream, you can only watch. The scene plays over and over, the scene of leaping girls, floating girls, one girl unable to leap. Her feet stick to the ground. Sometimes in the dreams, the girls are as tall and thin as cornstalks. Bellies sucked in, concave. Each pelvis, clearly outlined. You imagine a Georgia O'Keeffe, bleached sunlit bones, infinite blue horizons. What happened to soft belly flesh? Sometimes the girls dance until their hair falls out in clumps. Nobody notices what they have lost. Above them the dance instructor hovers like a dark star. The girls rise and hover too. One night you, too, rise with his command, gliding upward as naturally as a kite being sucked by a gust of wind. The dream is gone as suddenly as it came.

The Cat

When I was a girl, I lived on a farm where bears wandered in the woods. *They're just berry-eating bears*, my mother said. *Nothing to be afraid of.* But there were bobcats, too, that slunk in the leafy shadows of tree limbs. Once, when I was four years old, I looked up and saw one, as huge as a tiger, looking down at me with yellow eyes.

That night I dreamt I was eaten by a tiger. *How did he eat you?* a therapist asked years later. Slowly. That's how. He kept me alive night after night, licking the salt from my fingers and tears and the nape of my neck until gradually he became my mind. He became my fears and the song of my thoughts like the soft padding of slippered feet as I walked the hallways on sleepless nights. He became the absence inside me long after he left, a faint sensation, like tiny claws just beginning to sink into my gut and groin. It's that feeling I came to define as being alive.

❧

Lying

Those days it was an art, a way of closing up those small wounds, taking the whole world inside and letting it burn. Nobody was there to set the record straight, all those lies trapped inside us like a silent movie we'd keep on living in just as long as we could. If anyone ever asked, we said *yes Ma'am* and *fine* and *it sure is, thank you* or *pretty good*. Nights we'd ride our bikes over to Milton's Pond for a cool swim, then lie back in the tall grass, watch the summer triangle rise overhead, our lips touching places we'd say we'd never been.

The Portable Pussy

Wherever I go, I carry a pussy with me. How, you might ask, but I and the pussy are not one and the same being, so carry it I must. Asleep or awake, depending on who else is in the room, the pussy talks. Quietly of course, so as not to attract attention or disturb the peace. And honestly, much too honestly, really. I am so relieved when those who hear it pretend not to. Or perhaps they imagine they are only hearing things. On rare occasions the pussy gets carried away. Then it sings off-key or starts composing poetry. Of course, most don't suspect (or so I hope) that it's the pussy and not I who sings, or how difficult it is to carry a pussy everywhere I go, much less listen to the running commentary when all I wish is silence. A little relief. I even sought medical advice, but the doctors insist the pussy is all in the mind. I need only stop thinking about it, and the pussy will vanish forever. So I have been thinking about not thinking about the pussy. But I have fears. If the pussy is in my mind, alongside my thoughts, what if the thoughts leave first? If I have to pick between a pussy and a brain, which will it be? After all, who can choose between the player and his flute? The sea below and the sky above? How can I ignore *the gullies for the torrents of the rain and the path of the thunderbolt*? And who am I to command the waves *thus far and no farther shall you come.*

❧

The Accidental Seduction

One summer I took up watching a stranger in a nearby apartment building as he checked out the stars every night after sunset. Each time when I opened my windows and saw him gazing into the light-polluted air, I called out his name, *Luther, Luther.* He never heard. At least he never turned to look. It was unbearably hot that summer. I wore only sleeveless nightgowns that clung to my skin like Saran wrap. Whenever he turned, ever so slightly, I waved my nude arms wildly. Despite my efforts, Luther never noticed. Maybe, I thought, his name isn't Luther after all. (In fact it wasn't, but he liked the name well enough and later said it would do fine.) One evening, when I caught sight of a comet, trailing blue flames and vanishing behind the building across the street, I jumped on a trapeze. I swung across the alley, landing noiselessly on his terrace. He was remarkably surprised and quite delighted to show me his personal view of the heavens. That night the comet swept so close our arms and legs were singed by its tail. I still have red marks on my left shoulder blade and wrist.

❧

Satori

Sometimes I would imagine you, standing outside in the dark, peering in the lit yellow windows. I could feel your eyes on my skin, or something soft moving down my arms like pinpricks of rain.

Often I felt so lost, I didn't know where to turn. I had no faith in psychics, weathermen, or shrinks who think they can predict the future. Instead, I would hang out in the waiting room of loss, watching my loss, contemplating loss, not yet living my lost life.

Sometimes at night I became a moth, moon-bathing on your screens, pressing my soft brown wings against the metal.

When I dreamt of you, you were a stranger, but everywhere you touched me left imprints on my skin, like fingerprints in snow, like tongue marks in frozen custard.

Once, when a lover pressed his ear to my chest, he heard, not a heartbeat, but the silent cries of drowning.

I remember the last time you told me, *I am into Zen. I am transcending desire.* But whenever I made love, I could hear you, calling and calling my name, drifting and wheeling overhead.

One day, I know the barrier between us will lift. The loss will become me, and me, lost. That will be my satori. Nothing more.

Any Kind of Excuse

It happened so slowly, I hardly noticed at first. The way you moved me step by step out of my past, my town, my self. Separating me from everything visible, everything that said yes. Of course I tried to get a grip, to hold onto some strand or word. I made up any kind of excuse. But that meant nothing in the end. Outside the streets and stars took quiet walks alone. The mornings after you left, the sea unrolled one wave at a time, like hair falling loose from a clasp. You were all around me then, you and this loneliness like a dream, like a dress, like a sea or a shadow of the sea lifting in waves from the palms of my hands that remember your skin, the nape of your neck, and the curve at the base of your spine. In those days I wore nothing beneath my silk dress. You brushed my hair over my shoulders again and again, watching it separate around my shoulders and breasts. When you kissed me even the room kept watching. You could not stop. I still can't, no matter what you say. Or said.

Déjà Vu

The first time I met you, I knew you would leave me. It would happen suddenly, perhaps on a Thursday. Already I possessed the memory of it. An autumn evening spent like so many drab moments, tiny gray ones, followed by weeks of shadows. Perhaps it occurred while watching each other through a haze of exhaustion and cigarette smoke, at dusk in some dingy restaurant, the candles sputtering, and outside, rain gushing through the drainpipes, winged maple seeds spinning past our window. We didn't even notice the change at first. Everything looked so tired. Even the apartment buildings looming across the street like lit honeycombs kept closing their shades. And the truth is never obvious anymore. Why should it be? Habit prevents us from noticing the subtle changes—the feeling that everyone is holding his breath, like the hush when a symphony stops playing, and nobody blows his nose. We hear in the orchestra, not Mozart or a drum beat, but the drip of a faucet. Each drop is our universe, waiting to fall.

❧

The Kiss

At first I thought it would be simple to forget. To become a nun, leave it all behind, that life we never lived, though it hovered above me in the summer air. That's how I learned. The mind is but a door. Anyone can come in, especially you. Days passed, so many of them, and in each one I saw you again and called your name like a chant, a song, a prayer. Soon I became so used to you, leaving your trace in my mind, like a shadow on the sea, a sea of shadows. Only the birds kept watching, lifting me each morning out of my darkness. In my misery I smoked cannabis, drank wine, went pale and cold. I grew so lonesome, even my pubic hair turned gray overnight.

After a while, I became an insomniac. Doomed to stay awake in my tiny red room, night after night, reading sacred texts on what the saints never said, I studied recipes for insight and the end of remorse until finally I gave up and simply stared into space. I watched the moon and planets and traveling stars. In the end I knew but a single fact. The past is in the present no matter what I do. It moves beneath my fingers and the tips of my pens. It's what I worship, what no one can resist. Those windswept deserts and promised lands, that manna, that bush of burning bliss.

How I envied you, then, and all men like you, who float like milkweed in the wind, wandering through random cities, cities full of houses, houses full of rooms, rooms bleeding light in the darkness, the scope of their thoughtlessness extending infinitely outwards in a shimmering, an envelope of light, before vanishing forever.

The Magic and Mystery of an Empty Street

At last the day arrives when I glance out the window and see you leaving, that vanishing point where the street no longer holds your image and not even a shadow bleeds from your feet. That's when I remember a picture my mother owned called *The Magic and Mystery of an Empty Street*. But it was not an empty street. It was a painting of a girl, rolling a Hula-Hoop down a sidewalk, a girl so alone I could hear her breathing, but she could never see me, no matter how hard I stared. Absorbed in the Hula-Hoop, she didn't even notice the sun beating down on her head, making it hot like the flat of an iron. Even her hair smelled like summer and lemon cream rinse. Her hand, balanced lightly on the top of the hoop, kept rolling the hoop down the pavement and around the curve of the street, rolling and rolling. No matter what happened, she could never let it fall.

❧

Pepper Facts

It's true what they say. A certain kind of spice can get under a woman's skin. Once ingested, she will sweat it for days. She will taste it in the air and on her sheets; she might feel as if she were living in a Mexican restaurant. The scent can take ages to leave once the heat is in her blood. For a while a woman might think it's the man she's sleeping with, that he's gotten inside her clothes and every cell she is. Chilies are potent, no doubt about it; some contain antibiotic properties, inspiring a fire to rise in the blood, replicating the sensation and biochemistry of romance. A woman will lie awake, tossing and stirring, unable to sleep. She will eat bowl after bowl of ice cream beneath a full moon. But in the end she will discover it's nothing a little baking soda in her wash can't cure. And what a relief she will feel then! She might howl at the stars. Or dance nude in a snowstorm, her arms flung wide to the wind and singing cold, happy at last to be listening to her own thoughts that promise her, *never again. Never again.*

When a Woman Loves a Man

I was eating scones and sipping espresso at the Café Arabica when I learned of my love affair with you. Everyone has been talking about it, though it came as news to me. Good news. I had no trouble believing every word.

True, I have no idea what you are like in bed. Yet I'm convinced I need only lean back in my chair, gaze out the window and incline my thoughts toward you to remember, as if it were yesterday, the night I spent at The Top of the Town in Detroit, Michigan, staring down at the city lights.

Or was it several nights in Paris, or Venice, or Toledo, Ohio?

Perhaps the first time, you were wearing a Hawaiian shirt and those salmon pants you can barely squeeze into. It was only five o'clock in the afternoon. All day I'd spent dressing and undressing.

How I worry about my lovemaking. I who know so little about such matters. Were my kisses tender enough? Did I, as the street musician played the harmonica outside the window, unzip my azure dress, my breasts floating about as two clouds in a brassiere, before sailing out the window?

Even the irises quivered in the breeze. Seeds of albizzia blew across the sidewalks. When I touched your face, I said I had never been seduced before. Then I bit all the buttons off your shirt, and spat them across the room like seeds. I took off your socks with my teeth.

I didn't rush you, did I?

Were you turned off by my voluminous Woolworths underpants? I never could find them again. Perhaps you will mail them back some day.

Afterwards I slipped out without even saying goodbye, wearing the jacket from your Pierre Cardin suit and your wedding band, which I tossed to Marcel, the mustachioed bellboy with hair the color of honey. He slid it on his ring finger and blew me kisses as I sashayed out into the night.

Shivering, I turned only once, waved and tossed a handful of pebbles at your darkened window, and shouted your name and *I love you* again and again at the top of my lungs.

I told no one about this. I have no clue how the word got out.

Man-thing

I kept that man-thing for months until he grew thin as a sliver and green on the outside. I even let him rest on the windowsill, fed him sunlight, views, and vitamins. Daily he sipped plant juices. On occasion I took him out for entertainment, showed him to friends. I could tell what they thought by their blank stares. After a while, his presence irked me. He made sucking noises when he slept. His breath smelled of a cabbage garden. Each day I could stand him less. Still, he offered himself up. When winter came, I left him out on the patio. The stem of the man froze to an icicle. I pulled him out like a splinter and, with a distant clinking sound, he shattered. Perhaps it hurt a little. I can't be certain.

Male Logic

I finally had to face the facts. Men believe in logic. Control. Only a man would tell me, as you often did, *It's the thought that counts.* Not my body or the lavender dress I am wearing or the day of the week or the words of my dreaming pussy, the ones, I am so sorry to say, you never heard. But they are all the same, Love. What I think is in my body and clothes and words. No matter how often I told you this, you never understood. One day, I gave up and said, *Listen, Honey, I'm sorry. Maybe I'm just having a bad day.* That's when you gave me that tape entitled, *Reason Your Way To Bliss.* I tried to listen to it. Honestly, I did. But I stopped, every time, at the point where the speaker (a man, of course) was saying: *If you take a rock and examine it beneath a microscope, it is no different from a human beneath a microscope. Everything is just atoms and molecules. But can a rock have a bad day? Can a bad day be seen beneath a microscope? Of course not. If a rock is smart enough not to have a bad day, then how could you be having a bad day?* I had to turn off the tape. This, Love, is male logic at its best.

❧

Black Magic

He said, according to William James, there are laws in psychology. If you form a picture in your mind of what you would like or wish, and you hold that picture long enough, you produce what you are thinking. In this way monks in certain Himalayan monasteries manifest women out of thin air while balancing cups of steaming gooseberry tea on their cocks. I understand this now, he said, and all the laws of psychology. And how my thoughts have been traveling beneath your skin. Sometimes you hear them in dreams or at dusk like the drip of a faucet or the evening news. You can't rest at all, much less sleep. Of course, you might try to resist, but it's as hopeless as a prayer, clinging to the impossible. In a matter of minutes, you are lifted from the bed or couch and out on the streets, your dress quivering in the wind like a loose sail. Strangers watch you go. They don't know how it happens, a woman suddenly following the darkened streets, perhaps even flying on wings. Nor do they understand the danger of it, and that it is I who am to blame. Or how it feels to fly, the fear, the lack of control, that sensation like new teeth cutting into the shoulder blades. When you arrive, knocking on my door, there's always that first moment when you might plummet from the air, and feel my thoughts wash over your body like a loving glance or a cold stare.

He said, you've become a mere figment of my imagination, a silhouette, lit by my mind. Or my own grief. I even know what you fear. The day I will say to myself, *This woman is not all she's cracked up to be.* The day you'll think, *This man is a real son of a witch.* And the flicker of anger singes our skins. That's always the beginning, the taste of bitterness and salt, when we first lick the surface of our tiny black hearts.

❧

Always Have a Joyful Mind

How did I ever stand it? Those little sayings. Platitudes. The kind you always delivered, as if they were vitamins or the elixir of life. Take: *Beautiful thoughts make a beautiful day.* Or: *Always have a joyful mind.* As if I could live like an ant in honey. As if my mind could stay in one place forever, a tiny lit room, a strip of beach, sun-drenched skies. As if there were no one else, no strangers sleeping in your room. As if my lips were made of rose petals, and the sound of my thoughts was Pachelbel's canon, playing on repeat. As if sadness did not cling to my skin like a fine yellow dust. As if, just once, if only for a moment, that tiny thread connecting me to this earth—to the wine in my teacup, to the phone that stops answering me, to the street below where I see you walking through the winter snow, the rainy sidewalks, the sunlit cabs—could be cut as easily as *snip, snip,*

and I would ascend like Mohammed's horse, like the rider of Mohammed's horse, or the angel of the rider of Mohammed's horse, or the halo of the angel of Mohammed's horse, a bright ring of light glimpsed for a moment by you, my dearest,

yes, you. But I'd never notice. I'd be so far above you as I filled the horizon and beyond.

Asuncia

Now that you are gone, I am so lonely, even the angels love my sorrow as if it were their own. Sometimes I imagine them, reclining at beach resorts or walking the streets of their glass cities or descending in silver jets to survey the miseries of earth they admire so.

Only they can see or hear me, now that I refuse to go out, now that any illumination would be gratefully accepted. But insights, I think, are only occupied by angels for certain hours of the summer light.

During the winter months the dark ones sip absinthe and stick pins in our hearts. I feel them like a twinge or ache I can't resist. Just last night while drinking my third glass of cheap Chablis, I heard one whispering, I thought, the word *Asuncia*.

That's how they always speak, in single words with several or no meanings. *Asuncia,* I pondered, wondering if that were some city in Paraguay or a cathedral in downtown Cleveland, the art of levitation, a flavor of liqueur like anisette, or the name of a Spanish saint or poet like Vallejo.

Yes, like Vallejo whose grief was a kind of sex all women would die for in a single night.

If only I could die like that. I picture him, Vallejo, my own Vallejo, his soul enveloping me, gently at first, like a mist. *Asuncia, Asuncia,* he whispers again and again until I rise above the clouds. Such bliss could blaze through eternity, I assure you.

You who were good for a mere matter of minutes.

Crossing

Suppose the dead can't help looking back, pressing their wings against the glass like giant moths as if they don't get it, that the flesh is a cell, the light a 50-watt bulb. Maybe this dim life of regret is heaven after all. Like seeing you again at dusk, or imagining I do, there in the shadows of pines leaning through my windows, your arms waving in a frantic dance. When you kissed me, my back arcing like a bow, I remembered thinking the last kiss is always the best. I read that in a book about Tibetan monks who were paid to practice dying, to come back with news. After a while death became as familiar as a shirt slipped on or off. A kind of love affair, the monks discovered, an unspeakable intimacy. Some monks discovered a death that is just the right size, an ocean designed for the palms of their hands, each thimble-sized wave preparing for flight. Occasionally, one got stuck on the other side. Unable to touch the living or leave for good, he would call for help again and again, flailing his arms like the drowning, inhaling the ache in the distance between heaven and earth. I know how he felt, his silent cries, hot pebbles in the back of his throat.

❧

My Houdini

This is not a place to begin. Maybe there never is one. I take notes, measure your absence. A whiteout, a puff of smoke, Muzak. Maybe it's enough to know you are lingering in the silence I hold. The word *wistful* floats to mind. Wisting you here. Sometimes I say, *Hello, you*, mess up your hair into a wild rose. Make a list of all I need. Cinnamon. Cilantro. Sense. But it's too late now. Everything's so closed. The hours are trapdoors. Whatever falls through falls. Too hot to sleep. Or cold. I want to know how long one night can last. Pretend we're the only two people ever. Offer you a slice of tangerine. Here at the end of the universe on these stone steps.

**

It's true I feel a little tinge or suspicion after the fact. A sudden wind, a door blown open, your breath on my neck. Be prepared, I tell myself. Slowly, I learn. How to pin down a shadow, press you to the floor. Each time, I get a little bolder. Pulling you inside like a breath I won't let go, breathing in and in, into that breath behind each breath . . . until I feel that snap of some little bone spur or spring in the heart that lets things flow again. Afterwards I stare out the window at the lake, a shimmer racing across my surface. I pretend to look at whatever I am looking at.

**

Of course that was years ago. And now? Who is that woman? I see her entering your apartment. I see her walking in the shadow of the tall buildings on Chagrin Boulevard, looking just like me. Artsy, well-dressed, smart. Shockingly blonde. Sometimes I want to say, *Stop!* Make her look at my eyes. See? This one, green. This one, a little darker green. Runs in my family, two shades of green. Every night I stare in the mirror to see if it's still true. I talk to myself, too. *Sweetheart?* I ask. *Have you stopped sleeping? Well, me too.* I used to think a woman has choices. Love is one. But it's not. The first time you meet someone you love, you're already in love. You're already undressing him. And you aren't the only one. It's the damnedest thing.

Sleeping with Houdini

for Lynn Luria Sukenick

One of his best tricks is disappearing at will. Suddenly we are gone. We watch the world without us in it, like a paperweight full of snow falling. A body can do whatever Houdini wants and then chat with the birds. Birds can forecast the future. They can tell tomorrow's weather and the next president and the day a soul must leave. Houdini and the birds can undo things too. Like a blouse with the past inside. Like a stranger I sobered up beside and quickly unkissed. Like dying. I tried it in an oven and a noose, and each time it was the same slow sliding into bliss. Just when I thought the show was over, I woke up on soft flannel sheets, a heavy arm draped over my hip. The problem is, everyone falls in love with death. Death is the most seductive lover. Everything a person wants, death has.

III
The Beautiful Lie

Twenty-seven in a Row

One morning at the Café Arabica, a lady told me she knew a woman who had 27 consecutive orgasms. I didn't believe a word of it. Insisted it was a mere case of hypothetical ecstasy. I knew. The evidence of falsehood? The lady was counting.

Still I imagined a row of 27 erect penises arriving on a conveyer belt. Like sheep, the penises were counted. And viewed as a kind of delicacy. Perhaps in Technicolor. Large pink plants. Some were pale pink, and some fuchsia. My mother always said well-fed tulips produce a deeper color. Factory plants, grown under fluorescence, are never satisfying. They reminded her of cafeteria foods that taste dank. And need butter.

Did the lady play leapfrog? Was it a multi-penis man? I suggested at least five penises waving like a hand. The woman wondered what brand it might have been. Or was it a body builder with a muscular tongue? I suggested a singular penis and a lady who counted during sex. We don't know where it lives. Besides, it might be burnt out by now.

A man who was eavesdropping questioned the feminine potential for excessive climaxing. Could it be harmful? He argued a lady with 27 orgasms would have to be a ravaging sort, not like the woman who lived next door. No, this was a greedy, conquering sexual Napoleonette. We could hear her then, like a low wind, irreverently howling, moaning, calling our names. The man held his ears.

I was unafraid. I had other ideas and an analytic mind. The penis, I've determined, should never be overrated. No doubt our lady of the orgasms was hooked to an array of pulsing wires. Her naked body displayed on a medical table, covered only by a thin white sheet of paper. She rested, shivering in the sterile air on this contemporary altar as doctors watched. The experimental results will be sold in a new and startling book on female superiority. Did the doctors despair? Now, with electricity, there are no limits. But what did they discover? Sorcery. A black magic. A spiral dance into a woman without end.

Zen 101

The first time it occurred to me there are no orgasms in this world, I was studying Buddhism. My teacher had told me I don't exist. I am not solid, not even here. I both haven't arrived yet and am already past, already tomorrow, already gone. I had no clue what he meant, so he gave me a koan, something about who was I before I was born. An orgasm, I said silently, just waiting to happen. Suddenly I pictured all the orgasms in the universe, floating overhead like clouds, like angels.

Don't ask me why, but I pictured them all as women, nudes in many shapes and colors, like the nudes I examined in a girly magazine once at Sammy's Quick Stop. The man behind the counter was talking about the Red Sox, not noticing me. The first article I read promised the orgasm I've never had, and 5 new ways to win HER back. I wondered what she looked like, which she was of the photos inside. I flipped through the pages. I kept flipping and flipping. So many women looking enchanted, lit beneath a spotlight, little starlets, some wearing nothing but wings. I couldn't believe they were real. I imagined each to be exactly the size of the photograph, maybe 5 by 7 at most, tiny caged women with velvet eyes. Without their cages I'm sure they would fly away, and I wanted them to.

There was something so frightening about seeing them tiny and bound. I couldn't get them out of my mind, their wet lips and thighs. I kept thinking maybe the photographer painted the negatives, adding color and shine. Of course, I decided there are no women like that, and no orgasms like the promised ones. They left town ages ago. Though each time I make love, I close my eyes (I can't believe I'm confessing this), and I see one of those silky blondes, or the brunette with ringlets dangling beneath her breasts, her half-opened cat-eyes looking back or down at me with disdain, as if to ask, *Why are you wasting my time?* Then she sticks out her tongue. By the time I've opened my eyes, she's gone. And I can never decide which of us is merely a mirage. She? Or I?

Two Lives

We each have two lives. One to live by. One to die by. Every twenty minutes, one becomes the other. One quits, goes quiet. The secondhand on your watch sticks. And inside the heart a hole opens. At first the stop is tiny; and the hole, a pinprick. A pause, a gasp, a sigh. But gradually the hole expands until one day it becomes a door that swings wide. That's when a stranger walks through. When you look up, you might ask, *Do I know you?* And maybe you do. Maybe he's your first love or some guy who died of an overdose once upon a time. He never says hello. He watches you watch him before he leaves without a word or a second glance.

Maybe he thinks, *Yep, that's life. That's what it was like.*

The Divorce

After the papers were signed, after I knew I was a single woman at last, I felt what it means to be alone for the first time. I felt as if everything were many sizes too big. Even the view of the sky overhead, divided by pine trees. It could go on and on forever. That's what I kept to myself. I stayed inside. I needed to feel how the air slipped around me, and the sheets, too. And my own skin, how it wrapped around each finger and hipbone and traveled down my spine. I liked it, the perfect fit of my single body. And how I could place it, just so, in any hour and room like a single stalk in a glass vase.

❧

The Aftermath

After we made love, I couldn't stand you. I needed you to leave. I needed you to leave again and again, and each time you left, you were more in my life than ever before. Until at last, when you were truly gone, I saw you everywhere. You were in the sheets I slept in, the water I washed with, the shirts and pants I slid into. Until there was no part of me you didn't touch, no breath or pulse you didn't feel, no place you would not kiss, no bliss you called enough. Until you were in the silence too, when the words were no longer visible, when they no longer held what meaning means. Until you were no more than a memory. Even then you were touching me. Even then. And after. And after that, too.

Shadows

It's late, a Tuesday evening. I am at my desk, working, and you are here again. Maybe you don't even notice how you are leaning against my ottoman, sipping Perrier, staring past me and out the window. Even the birds can't resist you. They come in just to fly around your head, to inhale your aroma of shaving cream and sadness. I don't want to say exactly what I am doing with you, or thinking, even what you are wearing (you rarely bother much with clothing these days), though you look stunning against the red wallpaper. I always wanted to take you home, let you rest among my furnishings. I don't even know how long it's been since I found your journal, the one you lost once upon a time, but for days I've done nothing but read it from cover to cover. It's been almost a social occasion. I am finding your voice again, at last, and after all these years. And it speaks to me. Yes, it does. Sometimes I wonder if you ever left at all. Maybe we only imagine time and distance, though I have to admit, it has been ages since you phoned. I will write my name and number on the right hand side of this page, just in case you forget.

The Ideal Survey

He calls every evening between 6:00 and 7:30. What he really wants to know is something personal, such as *Are you easily fulfilled? Often alone? Is your life dictated by a luminous clock, a glass of Merlot?*

Do you have no choice? No second chance? How long have you yearned for something else, a little applause, a heyday to call your own, a device to minimize your worries or waist at a moment's notice, or an exclusive sense, a god for your own personal use, no one else's, as luxurious as a silk robe or sex after abstinence?

I'm sorry, he thinks, *maybe I should hang up, call another time, let you eat, simmer, smoke.* But he can't help himself. He persists but promises not to request your credit card. There is so much he wants to ask. He starts again:

Would you mind saying how many couches are in your den? Do you possess any small furry pets? Did you eat your beets? What is your recipe for bliss? Has anyone ever called you a mensch or a peach? Do you believe in the afterlife? A miracle found with a magnifying glass? If you had to pick between a watermelon and a Pekinese, which would it be? Do you itch? What if I called you my little bride? Beneath your bodice, does your heart hum like a honeybee? Do you sometimes wake to the rustle of wings? Do you think of life as soft and subtle like an instrument, played adagio, or is it always staccato?

On an ice-glazed morning, how long would you search for a cup of coffee or steaming tea? Do you like the scent of lemons or vanilla best? Do you wish you could croon like Mahalia Jackson? Or James Taylor? Do you feel easily diminished? A lack of rest?

Do sedatives bring sorrow or sing in your veins? What is the icing on your cake? Why are you never convinced? Do you agree with the following statement: a man pretends he's alive long after he's passed.

❧

My Life as a Spy

Once upon a time I had to travel to rogue nations. I was a spy, a kind of special envoy for the U.S. government, a part of the Secret Service called Operation Smart Blonde. My mission, to save the world. In preparation I dyed my hair platinum and bought several slinky outfits. I complained to my supervisor that I was too smart to be marketed in this way, to which he responded, *au contraire*. My job, he said, was to seduce a certain spiritual leader, whose name I can never confide.

Wherever he went, men with ski masks followed. I can't tell too many details, of course, this being a top-secret thing, but I was terrified. I felt as if my hair glowed like a light bulb in the limo in which the religious scholar and I were driven to an undisclosed location. When I asked where we were going, he answered, in his heavy accent, *All destinations are unknown*, and poured me a glass of something vile. He said it was some sort of wine, pressed from the fruit of a cactus. He asked if I knew the truth—why I was there.

Before I'd taken a sip, I admitted I'd studied philosophy and had once believed truth existed. It was the wrong thing to mention because he began to quiz me. All I could recall of philosophy were details of how certain philosophers related to women in bed. How, for example, Aristotle thought women were as interesting as shellfish. I drank rapidly in hopes the alcohol would give me inspiration. Soon I was babbling about Montaigne's theory of sexual impotence, Kierkegaard's fear and trembling, his dislike of his fiancée, Sartre's opinion that the best cake is never sliced. My head was spinning by the time I mentioned Descartes, and I couldn't even remember, *I think, therefore I am*. Instead I confessed, *I don't think like a blonde even if I am one, so forgive me*.

When I woke the next morning, I was blindfolded and gagged. A pair of callused hands fed and combed me and kept me underground. Nights I was bathed in almond oil and wrapped in blankets, transported across deserts and oceans by camels and planes. I expected to be rescued, but never was. So much time elapsed, I learned to see without eyes, to feel without touching, to hear without listening even the slightest flutter of an insect's wings. Slowly my hair faded to brown, and all their secrets became mine.

One night, I slipped free of my captors, leaving no trace. I walked alone and barefoot on sand-swept hills and cobbled streets, listening for footsteps. For the firm hand on my arm I would sense before it ever arrived. Without even suspecting it, I had transformed into a shadow of the woman, a memory belonging to someone else, perhaps a lunatic or ghost—or someone written off long ago, like Amelia Earhart, her plane blinking, then diving into the horizon like a firefly after summer is past. I boarded a ship that was departing for this country, stowed myself away, and arrived, safe in my own hometown, where no one would believe who I was or am.

Now, only I know what's at risk, and where and when and why. It is only I who understands the terrible truth and the future no one else foresees. I, a solitary woman with no name, no passport or formal ID, with all my history erased in order to secure my safety years ago. If only someone would listen. If only someone would believe. I am the last hope on earth. I, a skinny woman from the rural Midwest. Only I can save the world.

Zip Codes

The zeroes in your Manhattan zip code, 10003, are lonely women who feel the nothingness of existence. The one in the beginning is a single man, looking at the many zeroes, amazed by all the lonely, eager women. But the three at the end could mean trouble. Either in a family way or the way he goes for all three, attempting to make them all happy, but who can make a bunch of zeroes happy? One at a time, maybe, but he's not the kind to take it easy, to move slowly or cautiously. After all, he's a man from New York City. Notice, by contrast, 44122. No zeroes at all. People of zip code 44122 move in grape-like clusters. Overnight the twos become fours, separating years later into somber twos, walking side by side to the symphony on snowy January nights, falling asleep in their seats, only to waken years later to clap for the performance of a lifetime they never heard. The poor 1 in the middle is miserable among all those even numbers. He might be wise to consider moving to zip code 22903 where the nine, the largest zip number possible, is clear evidence of orgiastic sex, drugs, booze, cock fights, and nude women with gold-capped tits, slow dancing to country western music. At 22903 debauchery is an everyday event occurring beneath the veneer of an elegant society where twos live in white-pillared houses and talk in hushed voices about the horrid heat and the ghastly things this world is coming to. The zero and the three at the end are the woman who refuses to enter the antiquated tradition of matrimony, and the marriage she completes in the role of mistress and accomplice to the wealthy, southern gentleman whom she will blackmail when he runs for election next year.

❧

The Bed and I

after Henri Michaux

After you left, I saw you everywhere. I caught glimpses of your face in cafés and on passing buses and trains, even if it's true, you said you'd never come back. I kept hearing your footsteps behind me, and turning quickly, expecting to see that smirk on your face, your brown eyes looking down at me as if to ask, where have you been? I even started taking my bed with me, just in case. I wanted to be ready. Prepared. But after a while I wondered if you'd changed. Maybe you'd shaved your head, grown a mustache, lost weight. Maybe you'd started dressing up in coats and ties, taken a job in sales. You left me no hints. No forwarding address. Of course by then I'd tossed out all your bills. Your personal mail I read. To a few I wrote back, like your old pal, Ned, the one who prided himself on being an athlete in bed (he is) and that woman, Louise. I called her once. We agreed about you and a few other things. She said she was canceling plans to meet you in Madrid. Instead she's joining me for coffee at the Flaming Ice Cube next week.

After a while, how can I explain it? Every man I met looked like you. It didn't matter if his eyes were blue, if his hair was gray or if he was 5'3". No matter what he looked like or did, something went wrong. Something was missing. Each one left and left me with more to regret. Like this pain in my head, this ache in my bones. Maybe that's just what men do best. The mornings after I'd smell their sweat and cigarettes. There were stains on my carpet and on my furry toilet mats. I started avoiding the phone and the mail and took long trips out of town. I stopped seeing you (and everyone else, too) everywhere I looked. Of course you who know me might think this impossible. Now all my days are good. Nights it's just me and the bed.

The Beautiful Lie

Once I interviewed a famous poet. I won't say his name because it's a secret that I've kept so long, I can't just let it go. Besides, it embarrasses me. I was young then, younger than I ever knew, just out of college and infatuated with fame, and all dressed up in black silk and heels and a few dabs of cologne—I was really afraid, too. I thought he'd be this masterpiece of a man, a kind of soul that comes only once in a century. I'd read as much, so I wasn't prepared for the real thing.

He was late. Hung over. Stinking of old socks and cigarettes, he chewed gum because I said, *Please don't smoke, it gives me a headache*, which pissed him off, so he wouldn't answer any of my questions at first. The ones I'd carefully penned ahead of time—about his work, whom he admired and what was he thinking when he wrote his most anthologized poem, but all he'd say was that he'd already answered those questions a thousand times before, that I could look up the answers in *Parnassus* or *APR*, *The Paris Review* or *The London Times* or *The New York Review of Books*. He was acting like such a jerk. I wanted him to cut it out. I wanted to say, *Kiss my ass,* or *Fuck you.*

But I wanted my one hour with a famous poet, which he had agreed to, to be the kind of thing I could write about, maybe even publish, and in those days I would do anything to get what I wanted. Back then I believed in going to extremes, even if it meant playing a fool. So I got down on my knees and begged. I sank down on the dirty carpet in front of his chair where there were a few old cigarette butts, and I told him how much it meant to me to have this chance, that there were just so many questions I wanted to ask, I'd even had a dream about him. In the dream he told me something that he'd never told another soul.

He looked surprised, as if he didn't quite know what to say. Suddenly he started to laugh. Then he stood up and went to this side table and poured some wine. Merlot, and he gave me a glass, which I was grateful for, even if it was 10:00 in the morning. I sure needed it. He swallowed two glasses in two gulps, gazed at me for several minutes and sat down. When he started talking, again, he spoke fast—so fast I couldn't keep up with him, but I scribbled what I could. He said his favorite subject in school was recess; his favorite star, the one he just slept with; his favorite phone, the kind that never rings. He loved drugs, sedatives, sleep, and he could love his interviewer, too, if she'd let him, and he winked and put his hand on my knee, which gave me the creeps, but I kept taking notes, calling him an arrogant sad sack in tweed, and while I was writing he said he liked my blouse and pantyhose, which were black fishnets. I tried to steer him away from my legs by asking, *What do you think when you start to write a poem?*

That was when he changed, maybe because the wine was taking effect, making him melancholy, slowing him down. He didn't speak right away, and then he announced it as if it were his final sentence, *Lies. That's what I do. I make them up, one by one.* He said it's like slow-dancing with no one, not to do it, or to do it, and then he laughed and said something about how he was sick of being so fucking alone. He knew I was beating around the bush and that what I really wanted to ask was how I could become a famous poet like him, and that even though I wouldn't know it yet, he was doing me a favor by telling me. I had to learn someday. How to lie. Lie beautifully. Lie convincingly. Lie. And then he did tell his secret. The secret of the beautiful lie, the one he said I couldn't tell anyone, ever. Listen carefully, he advised in a whisper. And afterwards, he smiled, as if he were pulling my leg, and he might have been. He said he was too old. He didn't care about poetry anymore. He just wanted to drink. Make love. That's all. And so he did. Or we did. I can't be sure. It was a Thursday in Rome, New York. Or was it in Normal, Illinois? When I looked out the window, the streets were full of snow. I felt lonelier than I'd ever been. Nin Andrews is dead, I said to myself, and I knew it was so.

❧

Winging It

for Robert

Robert Bly said he was fed up with poems that just wing it, that don't connect to the things of the earth. He instructed everyone to write a poem in which they worshiped a thing or two, like an onion or a rock, and then ask forgiveness of the thing, or the God of the thing, so a writer might start out, *Oh rock, lovely rock,* and then he'd say, *Forgive me oh rock, for I know not what I do, dear rock* . . .

Then the poet would confess a sin or reveal something deep, profound, maybe dark, like the heart of a rock, the unseen depths and shadows lurking in the cold center of the rock, the undreamt dreams of the rock. . . . Or he might say how much he wished he were a rock, solid, unwavering, enduring. . . .

But whenever I started out, *Oh glorious rock,* and added *forgive me,* I got stuck, listening to everyone else's illuminating rock and onion poems, as if they had just discovered how rocks and onions are sacred, what with their little rock souls and onion souls, and suddenly their entire lives could be seen as the lives of rocks and onions, while my rocks and onions remained nothing but rocks and onions and things . . .

But I didn't want to give up. I wanted illumination, too. So I kept trying, starting my poems again, saying, *Oh glorious rocks and things,* or *Oh God of rocks and things, forgive me for seeing you as cold and gray and dull, just like rocks and things. I don't even like your dull old rocks and things. You who never loved my thing.* . . .

I'd have to confess something then, right then, if I were writing a Bly poem. To tell a secret, profound and maybe troubling. Maybe I'd tell how the first thing my parents did when I slipped out of the womb was look for my thing. Of course, I didn't have one. Everyone felt sorry because my folks had wanted a boy so badly. My parents tried to act as if it were just fine to have a girl. And sometimes my dad would say, *Kiss your elbow, and you'll turn into a boy*, and I'd try. I didn't want to be a boy, but my elbow could almost touch my lips.

And each time I tried for my elbow, I could almost feel something between my legs. It was an exciting game, but I don't want anyone to think I had penis envy. Oh no, I didn't want any boy things. I just wanted to see them and say, *God forgive me for looking*. Penises are something to see. No two ways about it. Boys with their penises bopping around naked under the sprinkler in the hot July sun. *Whing, whing*, my friend, Jimmy would sing as we did our Indian dance under the water, his penis whinging with him, and his friend Bobo's, too, and Jeremy Jones—JJ we called him. All those little penises like the plastic firemen Aunt Ada gave me for my fourth birthday, firemen with little red caps, and I'd say, *God forgive me for thinking my toys are penises*, because everyone knows little girls aren't supposed to think like that, but then, most little girls don't even try to kiss their elbows, and I almost did. And they don't do Indian dances with penises under the sprinkler either.

Or ask God to forgive them, even as they dance, even though I wasn't a bit sorry for doing it. For not wearing a stitch of clothing and watching the penises dance and saying forgive me again and again, and I will say it again, God, even if you are just an old God of rocks and things. Even if you never danced as a small freckled girl, naked on the grass, and saw the whole world with its whings, just whinging and whinging and whinging it.

Dear Confessional Poet,

How else can I say it? I hate what you do. You and your entire school. Ever since that Christmas ages ago when my parents gave me the complete works of Anne Sexton, and Sylvia, too. Like Princess Di, both of them, only the princess was in the right profession. Of course, in those days confessional was IN. Poems about my ugly face and big, bad daddy.

For some reason they remind me of the first time I went to an evangelical church. It was with my friend Mary Rose. She was just so sweet, she wanted to save me. After the service women gathered in this carpeted room called the library (without books), and one of the clergy asked us *to kindly tell a little tidbit or two about our wounds.* It was horrible. I was there. I can't tell you how horrible it was. As if on cue this blonde started sobbing and talking of abuse. Even her bouffant hair was trembling . . . Terrible tales of an alcoholic dad and what he did, and others chiming in, *Me too.*

When it was my turn, I couldn't think so I told how once upon a time, when I was a little girl, my mom hated shopping so much, she bought all my clothes two sizes too big. Even my underwear was huge. It came all the way up to my nipples, and my skinny legs hung out of the holes like spaghetti strands.

Thank you for sharing, everyone said. All I wanted to do was puke. I think everyone did. I think that's what sharing means. Mary Rose patted my knee and hissed, *Is that true?* Yes, I said, but I wished it weren't. I wished I'd lied. Later, that's what my professor said to do. *Why not,* he told an entire class: *Define the woman you aren't and live to tell about it.*

Book Jacket

It wasn't your book but the jacket. And the photo on the jacket. That's where I first saw you. And knew immediately. How everyone wants to be seduced by you. Perhaps it would have been wiser to have photographed someone else. To have left the space blank, insisted on being a man with no face. To have a lock of hair, or a large leafy plant covering your nose. To suggest, if nothing else, there is more than meets the eye. Maybe there isn't, but who would have guessed? And that's not all of it. No, it was the credits beneath your photo. The expectations. Standards. 50% chance of cloudiness. Now everyone knows how years of solitude drained your mind as if it were a cup of juice. That you possess the natural voice of the transcendent man, the dazzling demons of disabused wisdom, the hymn of humdrum existence. You're the Adam of the avant-garde, the Houdini of the heart, the confessional of the cock, the poet of poets who can reduce the entire universe to a few words or a tiny room, seen through a keyhole. That's where we made love, long before we met. I almost remember it, as if it were last night. There, where the possibilities were infinite.

❧

Advice About Angel Poems

Please be advised. You should not write angel poems. Ever. They are cliché. They have been *done* like death and sex poems. Like love and loss poems, only worse. That's why, when you wrote in your poem, *That night the angel was floating above me on gossamer wings*, I whited her out. The angel has lost her intrinsic value. There is no longer blood in her veins. Maybe there never was. Allen Ginsberg said that whoever controls the language controls the race. Angels should not be given control. Why? Because we don't know what an angel is. Even so, 75% of Americans believe an angel helps them. Most of them think angels are female. One said he could hear the beating of her invisible heart. Because he can't prove she doesn't exist, she might. It is possible we sublimate our angelic perception. I know, you say that you were just being poetic, but being poetic is like having a prospective lover who can talk about sex but will never take you to bed. Picture her, then, your angel, as milky white as the froth in your cappuccino. She can only speak seven words, and even those, she keeps to herself. Her lips are made of rose petals, you say. Blue roses. Her mind is a tiny lit room where she is at peace forever, like a bee in a blossom, an ant in honey. She has no worries because she will never die. There are as many hours in her days as eggs in a supermarket. Not even a poet can say how she feels inside.

❧

The Last Frenchman, or
What I Learned in High School French

L'amour

She still thought about him sometimes. And what her French teacher taught her about him. Maybe because she was lonely. Maybe because it was just safer, in the beginning, to think of seduction as something that only happened across the ocean. Her teacher told her that sex in France is not dirty, not like in America. It is as clean as freshly washed linen, hanging outside her city windows. She imagined it there, on the balconies of the world.

Il y a du monde au balcon, a French lover will say to you, the teacher said once, while laughing and brushing her hair over her bare shoulders, applying her lipstick. But you won't know what he means. Because all Americans are lazy and imagine they speak the only language there is. They arrive in Paris, knowing how to ask where the train station is or what time the plane leaves. But they don't know where to find a ticket to the French soul. *Ils n'ont pas de ticket*, the teacher would sigh. They don't even know it exists.

Le Bouche à Bouche

So often she heard her young French teacher boast about the superiority of the French. That everything French is better. The best in fact. French poetry, French bread, French wine, French souls. And French kisses, of course. There's nothing quite like them. That's how she pictured him, her French lover, like the deepest kiss she had ever felt. She who had never French kissed. Her teacher explained that while the French kiss as a matter of mere greeting, Americans hardly show emotion. They don't understand the importance of affection. *Ils ont un retard d'affection.* American men are such diminutive lovers by contrast, they vanish at the slightest touch. They should not exist, even in memory.

L'imparfait

Only the French soul is eternal. Why? Because for the French, everything is ongoing, even if it is *imparfait*. Because the past doesn't just disappear. Because wonderful things can happen at any moment, even yesterday. Because there is no such thing as a place without romance. Or a time called the end. Because there is no respect for laws, not of any kind. The French are born anarchists who drive the wrong way down one-way streets and smoke in front of the signs *DEFENSE DE FUMER*. Even old lovers live alongside the new as equal citizens of your dreams, and who knows when one might return to your doorstep in mid-afternoon with a bouquet of lilies? Like fine wines, flowers in France are selected carefully for every occasion. Each scent has a different meaning. Gentians for sorrow, clematis for dreamers, apple blossoms for jealousy. Yes, there is a cure for jealousy. A special kind of apple tree. It only blooms in France.

Y

Everyone needs a country like that. Somewhere. A comma in the mind, a caesura. Expressed simply as *y*, meaning *there*. A v with a tail. There where she had never been, but she knew she wanted it, the mystery of it. Where no one solved for mysteries. No one looked through keyholes. Not even the concierge. For the French, a secret is the only thing worth keeping.

It would be nice, she thought in algebra class, never to have to solve for y. Y would remain just another place where someday they might meet. That place where her thoughts often went. *J'y pense*, her teacher explained. A place to respond to with letters. Or a postcard with a message from X, not wishing one were here, but knowing she'd be there—someday.

She pictured it, there, as those photographs of the south of France where it is always summer, where one dines on coffee and croissants, wine and wishes, where one wears no bikini top, and the beaches are the color of honey. Where she made love 1001 times before she ever made love. To a Frenchman, of course. There has never been another quite like him.

On

That's because you have never found the right one, the teacher insisted when she complained about boys. That's why you must fly off to France. In France there are so many of them, so many wonderful men that the French say *on*, meaning one, meaning him, meaning you, meaning we, meaning them—meaning everyone. In France one is capable of doing things one might never think herself capable of doing. And feeling—those little feelings, like a thousand minnows swimming through her veins.

One never knows how it happens. It happens so naturally. So swiftly. Only in France. One simply wakes up one morning in another room, another town by the sea—another world altogether. The world of *jouissance*. It always begins with a few words spoken by a real Frenchman, or whispered in the dark. And never ends. Even the gods speak French.

Jouissance

One doesn't understand pleasure in America. One can't because one doesn't have the words for it. In English class, her teacher even told her that one cannot get wet from the word *water*. That there is a difference between words and reality. Even the great American novelist Melville said God's only message is silence. Maybe, she reasoned, there is an entire zone where words and people never meet. They can't. Because words have no fingers and tongues. Because words can never reach where we are. Unless we live in France.

Everywhere else on earth, her French teacher informed her, the world is speeding up. It was true. She saw it happening all around her on the streets of Manhattan. Everyone in a rush. Sometimes a person would fall behind, losing days and weeks of their own lives. Their bodies would hurry on without them and were sometimes swallowed by subways and never seen again. When she went out dancing, dancing and dancing, she could barely keep up with the beat. What if she too lost the rhythm, she worried. Sometimes she still dreamed of France, of vacations there, the kind her teacher suggested she take. There in the south of France where every dance is a slow dance. Two weeks in Provence, her teacher said, is a one-night stand in New York.

Politesse

The French, unlike Americans, know how to take care of a woman. Almost as soon as one arrives, the French teacher assured her, a Frenchman will find her. They are so gracious, the French. So caring. Right away he will recognize her. He will know she is lonely and in need of his services. He will invite her to dine with him, introduce her to his friends, his city, his favorite sidewalk café, his flat. It is difficult to know how to respond to such unexpected kindness. But beware. One must never bring wine to the Frenchman's house. By doing so, she will suggest he doesn't know what to serve, or when.

La Cuisine

It is impossible not to fall in love with him. A Frenchman knows so many things. *Surtout*, the teacher said, how to drive you mad with love. How does he do it? She might well wonder. Maybe she will think it's because of his tiny ass. Did you know that all Frenchmen have tiny asses? It's true. You might think he has the silky white ass of an angel. And the hands too. Because French hands are truly celestial beings, and as agile as pianists'. Such hands are always kept above the tablecloth. This is the French way. Like bees around flowers, the hands move above each delicacy, circling and descending. One, being an American, might hardly notice at first. Because Americans eat quickly without even looking up. They don't even know what to do with their hands. They are like lovers who make love with their eyes shut. You will learn, the teacher explained, that in France the body is not treated like a car that needs a quick fill at a service station. In France a meal can take hours, even weeks. An entire lifetime might pass while one is eating a French meal. To dine in France is like sucking the nectar from a blossom, one drop at a time.

Le Marché

After a meal like a meal in France, one may never want to go home. The day will come when inevitably she will begin to worry. What if the Frenchman abandons her?

Of course he will have to leave her sometimes, if just for a moment, maybe to purchase groceries for their dinner. Not only do Frenchmen cook, her teacher taught her, but they are gourmets. They serve their women only the finest meals. Never, for example, would a Frenchman serve casserole (*il n'est passe jamais à la casserole!*). Instead, he will insist on shopping carefully, purchasing the freshest ingredients for the perfect meal. He will purchase steaks at the *boucherie*, fish at the *poissonerie*, cheese at the *crémerie*, vegetables from the *marché en plein air*, pastries from the *pâtisserie*, bread from the *boulangerie*, wine from the *negotiant en vins*, perfume from the *parfumerie*, diamonds from the *bijouterie*, bonbons from the *confiserie*, flowers from the rainforests of Brazil, pearls from the Sea of Japan where he will dive nude with the pearl divers forty feet down. Alas, the Frenchmen are not known for their faithfulness. And they adore pearls. Those tiny moons, like teardrops, at the bottom of the sea. Some get lost down there and never reappear.

Of course, he will always promise to return soon, but who knows when soon will be? In his absence sadness clings to her skin. Sadness like a fine yellow dust. It is always yellow in France, especially the south of France where they vacation beneath an azure sky. Where angels vacation. Even angels make love there. It is impossible to know if one is making love to an angel. Like the Frenchmen, an angel loves his soft prison. He cannot help himself beneath an azure sky.

Se Manquer

Once she has been with an angel, or a Frenchman, nothing can continue as before. A girl will feel so lonely. In a moment of despair, while staring at the horizon, she will imagine she no longer belongs to this earth. She is a kite with no string, a cloud slowly dissolving, a memory of last night. She will picture the world without her in it. All the while the Frenchman will continue to buy groceries and serve exquisite meals. Such meals. That's why he must leave, she reasons, to gather just the right ingredients, again and again. And to serve, always to serve. Sometimes, if she thinks about it, she becomes jealous of the meals she hasn't eaten yet, the ones he will serve tonight or tomorrow night. Or the night after that. Sometimes she becomes so jealous of herself, she can't stand it. She looks in the mirror with contempt. Who do you think you are to be living in the air, as if you belong there, she asks.

That's why she must decide never to miss him. It is much too painful. *Il me manque*, she says instead, meaning he is missing from me, as if there's a space inside where the missing always dwell.

Of course, there is. That space where she and the Frenchman remain forever, eating and eating, wiping the little crumbs of croissants from our lips, dabbing the chocolate mousse on our cloth napkins, sipping and tasting wine as only the French can, knowing with the first drop upon the tongue which vineyard it came from, and which year it was harvested from their missing world.

It is important to keep a place for the Frenchman—a place set at the table or at least in the soul. Who knows when an angel will knock at your door? Who knows when a Frenchman will return? But this is a story with a sad ending. Because the French are members of a vanishing race. Their population is dwindling. There are so few real Frenchmen left. Consider their numbers—less than a minuscule fraction of the world's population. No one knows when they will be gone for good. Sometimes they stop and listen to their own steps vanishing behind them, or glance to check their reflections in shop windows or a lover's gaze, as if to ask, *Am I the last one?*

Sometimes she imagines he is watching her from above, from a window on the seventh floor perhaps. In France a window is a beautiful thing. Just look at the word, *fenêtre*. One can almost look out of it with the eyes of an angel, there beneath the rooftops. Meanwhile, below, the world rushes past. In here there is no one. Now that the last Frenchman is gone.

Acknowledgments

I am forever grateful to the Ohio Arts Council and to the editors of the following journals in which the poems first appeared, sometimes with different titles:

ACM: "Always Have a Joyful Mind";
American Letters and Commentary: "Sleeping with Houdini";
Artful Dodge: "The Portable Pussy," "Winging It";
Cimarron Review: "Zen 101";
Cream City: "Zip Codes," "Man-thing";
Diagram: "Burning Point";
DMQ Review: "Cats," "The Divorce," "The Aftermath";
Exquisite Corpse: "Twenty-seven in a Row";
Flights: "Falling," "Making the Sun Rise," "The Game";
5 AM: "Asuncia," "Shadows," "The Kiss," "Advice About Angel Poems," "Déjà Vu";
Gargoyle: "The Beautiful Lie";
Hotel Amerika: "My Houdini";
Indiana Review: "Book Jacket";
Midwest Quarterly: "My Life as a Spy";
Pearl: "The Last Frenchman";
Ploughshares: "Black Magic," "When a Woman Loves a Man";
Poet Lore: "Brown Apples," "The Accidental Seduction";
Poetry International: "The Invisible Girl";
Salt Hill: "The Tunnel," "Sleeping for Kafka";
Seneca Review: "The Last Frenchman, or What I Learned in High School French";
Spoon River: "Crossing";
Washington Square: "Pepper Facts";
Web Del Sol: "Male Logic," "Like This";
Whiskey Island: "Aspirin."

"Always Have a Joyful Mind" also appeared in *Great American Prose Poems* (Scribner, 2003).

"Dust" first appeared in the chapbook *Spontaneous Breasts* (Pearl Editions, 1998).

"The Ideal Survey," "Man-thing," "Twenty-seven in a Row," "Asuncia," and "The Portable Pussy" also appeared in *The Book of Orgasms and Other Tales*, which is only available in the UK (Bloodaxe Books, Ltd, 2003).

"Satori" and "Zen 101" also appeared in *America Zen, A Gathering of Poets,* (Bottom Dog Press, 2004).

"When a Woman Loves a Man" and "Déjà Vu" also appeared in Poetry Calendars 2006 and 2007 (Alhambra Publishing).

I would also like to thank BOA Editions, especially Peter Conners and Thom Ward, for publishing and helping me complete this book; Robert Carioscia, the artist, for creating the cover; my brilliant friend, Stephanie Strickland, for her insights and editorial help; and my husband, Jim, and my children, Suzanne and Jimmy, for everything.

About the Cover Artist

Robert Carioscia is a visual artist and graphic designer living and working in New York City. He has been featured in many gallery and museum exhibitions. Carioscia is the recipient of awards and honors such as The Grumbacher Award in sculpture, the Hechsher Art Museum Award in Painting, and fellowships from Yaddo and the Virginia Center for the Creative Arts. He has also received a series of public and private art commissions, most recently a permanent art installation at Columbus Circle subway station, commissioned by the New York City Metropolitan Transportation Authority *Arts for Transit Program*. You can find more of his work and information online at rcarioscia@verizon.net.

❧

About the Author

Nin Andrews received her BA from Hamilton College and her MFA from Vermont College. The recipient of two Ohio Arts Council grants, she is the author of several books including *The Book of Orgasms, Any Kind of Excuse, Why They Grow Wings*, and *Midlife Crisis with Dick and Jane*. She also edited *Someone Wants to Steal My Name*, a book of translations of the French poet Henri Michaux.

Colophon

Sleeping with Houdini, poems by Nin Andrews, was set in Adobe Caslon, a digital version modeled on the widely popular designs of William Caslon (1692–1766). The display font, Linoypte Didot Italic, is based on types cut by Firman Didot in Paris in 1783 and is characterized by abrupt changes from thick to thin strokes and hairline serifs.

The publication of this book is made possible, in part, by the special support of the following individuals:

Anonymous (6)
Jeanne Marie Beaumont
Nancy & Alan Cameros
Wyn Cooper & Shawna Parker
Gwen & Gary Conners
Susan DeWitt Davie
Peter & Sue Durant
Pete & Bev French
Robert Giron
Dane & Judy Gordon
Kip & Deb Hale
Patti Hall & Joseph Shields
Robin & Peter Hursh
Nora A. Jones in memory of Max N. Rogers
Earl Kage
Archie & Pat Kutz
Rosemary & Lew Lloyd
Irving Malin
Stanley D. McKenzie
Boo Poulin
Deborah Ronnen
TCA Foundation on behalf of MidTown Athletic Club
Mike & Pat Wilder
Glenn & Helen William